THE CRUNCHY KID SERIES

THE CRUNCHY KID

LEARNS THE

ALPHABET

Cursive Edition

Written by: Angela Harders

Illustrated by: ______________

Hello!
I'm Cam the Crunchy Kid!
Together, we will learn our letters!
But I need your help to add
some color to the pages.
Are you ready?
Let's go!

Aa

Arnica

Avocado

Apple Cider Vinegar

Can you draw a picture of your favorite thing that starts with the letter A?

Broccoli

Bb

Bee

Breastfeeding

Can you draw a picture of your favorite thing that starts with the letter B?

C c

Coconut Oil

Chia Seeds

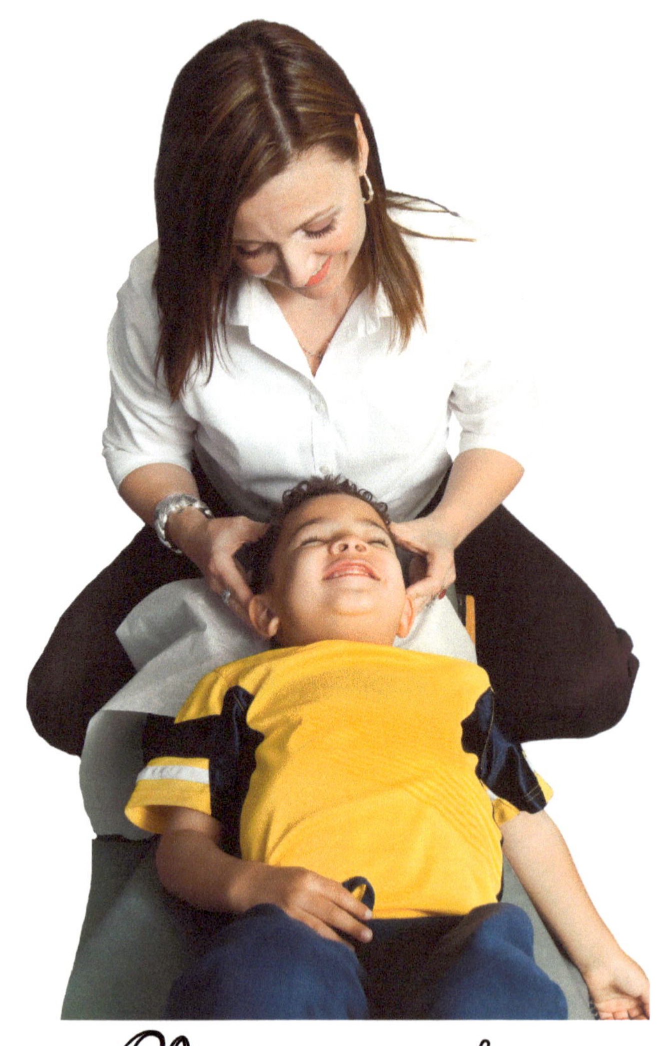

Chiropractor

Can you draw a picture of your favorite thing that starts with the letter C?

Dandelion

Dirt

Diffuser

Can you draw a picture of your favorite thing that starts with the letter D?

Ee

Can you draw a picture of your favorite
thing that starts with the letter E?

Frankincense

Farm

Friends

Can you draw a picture of your favorite thing that starts with the letter F?

G g

Ginger

Garlic

Grounding

Hummus

Hh

Healthy Food

Honey

Can you draw a picture of your favorite
thing that starts with the letter H?

Ii

Iodine

Invent

Ice Skating

Can you draw a picture of your favorite thing that starts with the letter I?

Jj

Juice

Jojoba

Jasmine

Can you draw a picture of your favorite thing that starts with the letter J?

K k

Kale

Kombucha

Kefir

Can you draw a picture of your favorite thing that starts with the letter K?

Lemon

Ll

Lion's Mane

Lavender

Can you draw a picture of your favorite
thing that starts with the letter L?

Mm

Mango

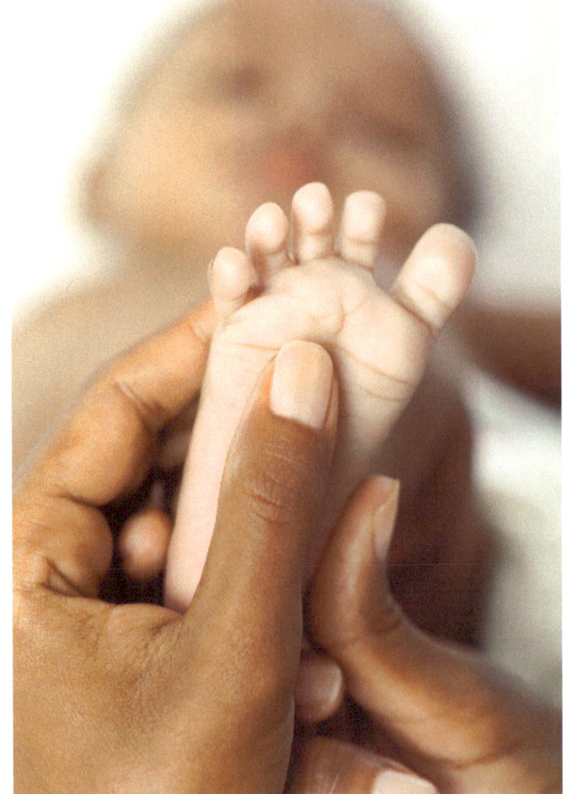

Mushrooms

Massage

Can you draw a picture of your favorite thing that starts with the letter M?

Nettle

N n

Neti Pot

Nature

Can you draw a picture of your favorite
thing that starts with the letter N?

Oo

Onion

Organic Food

Can you draw a picture of your favorite
thing that starts with the letter O?

Oregano

Pomegranate

P p

Pineapple

Parsley

Can you draw a picture of your favorite
thing that starts with the letter P?

Qq

Quinoa

Question Everything

Can you draw a picture of your favorite thing that starts with the letter Q?

Quiet Time

Red Raspberry

R r

Rose

Rest

Can you draw a picture of your favorite thing that starts with the letter R?

S s

Sunshine

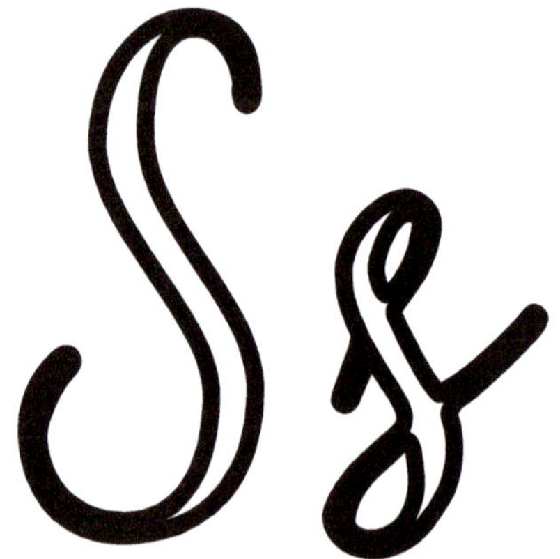

Salt

Can you draw a picture of your favorite
thing that starts with the letter S?

Sauna

Tumeric

Tt

Tomato

Time In

Can you draw a picture of your favorite
thing that starts with the letter T?

Uu

Usnea

Uva Ursi

Can you draw a picture of your favorite thing that starts with the letter U?

Unschooling

Vitamins

Vv

Vinegar

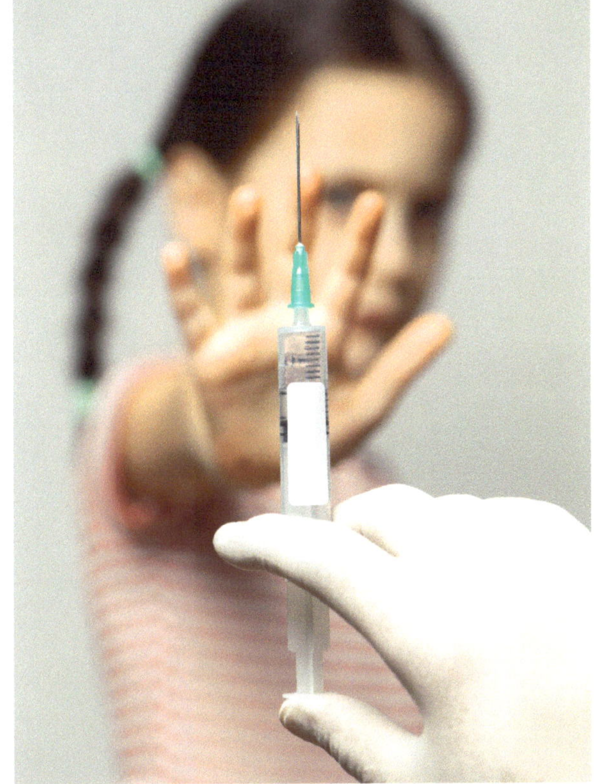

Vaccine Free

Can you draw a picture of your favorite thing that starts with the letter V?

Ww

Watermelon

Wonder

Can you draw a picture of your favorite thing that starts with the letter W?

Water

Detox

X x

Xanthan Gum

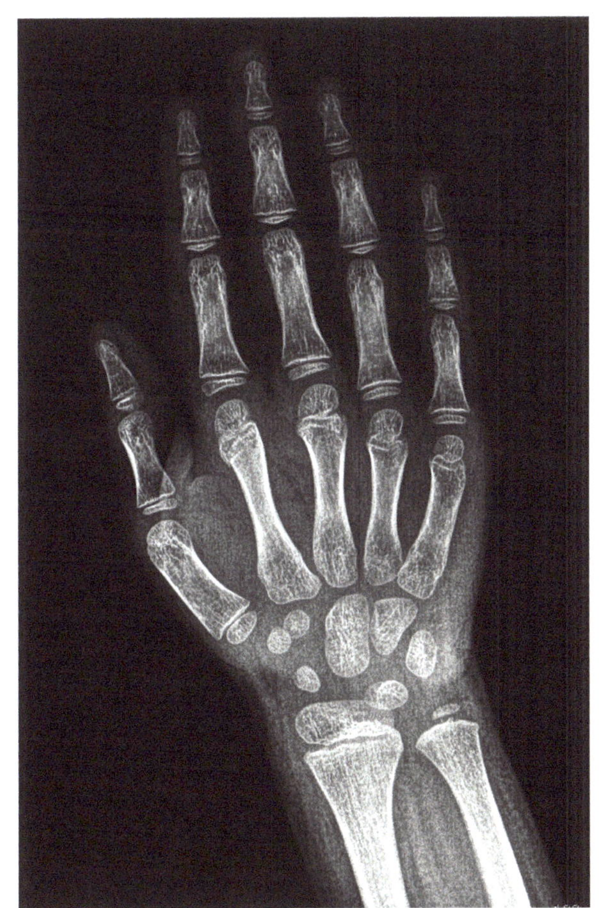

X-Ray

Can you draw a picture of your favorite
thing that starts with the letter X?

Yy

Yarrow

Ylang Ylang

Yoga

Can you draw a picture of your favorite thing that starts with the letter Y?

Zz

Zinc

Zucchini

Zinnia

Can you draw a picture of your favorite
thing that starts with the letter Z?

The Crunchy Kid Alphabet

Aa Bb Cc Dd Ee Ff Gg

Hh Ii Jj Kk Ll Mm Nn

Oo Pp Qq Rr Ss Tt Uu

Vv Ww Xx Yy Zz

WHO IS A CRUNCHY KID?

"Crunchy" is a word that describes a person who strives to live a natural life. You may do all of these things - or perhaps just one or two, but a commitment to physical, mental, emotional, and spiritual health and wellness is the biggest sign that you're a crunchy kid in a crunchy family.

Crunchy Kids usually love to...

- breastfeed
- wear cloth diapers
- use amber necklaces
- take Epsom salt baths
- eat raw, organic foods
- go to the chiropractor
- avoid putting toxins in/on the body
- co-sleep with family
- do elimination communication
- use natural remedies
- be in a baby sling or carrier
- play outside barefoot
- homeschool
- and more!

For additional resources, please visit: www.peacefulworldschoolers.com.